Wok and Roll

1500 Days of Flavorful Cooking at Home with Asian Stir-Fry Adventures for Wok Wonders to Spice Up Your Meals / Full Color Edition

Grace Kim

Copyright© 2023 By Grace Kim Rights Reserved

This book is copyright protected. It is only for personal use. You cannot amend, distribute, sell, use, quote or paraphrase any part of the content within this book, without the consent of the author or publisher.

Under no circumstances will any blame or legal responsibility be held against the publisher, or author, for any damages, reparation, or monetary loss due to the information contained within this book, either directly or indirectly.

Disclaimer Notice:

Please note the information contained within this document is for educational and entertainment purposes only. All effort has been executed to present accurate, up to date, reliable, complete information. No warranties of any kind are declared or implied. Readers acknowledge that the author is not engaged in the rendering of legal, financial, medical or professional advice. The content within this book has been derived from various sources. Please consult a licensed professional before attempting any techniques outlined in this book.

By reading this document, the reader agrees that under no circumstances is the author responsible for any losses, direct or indirect, that are incurred as a result of the use of the information contained within this document, including, but not limited to, errors, omissions, or inaccuracies.

Editor: AALIYAH LYONS

Interior Design: BROOKE WHITE

Cover Art: DANIELLE REES

Food stylist: SIENNA ADAMS

Table Of Contents

Introduction

In the symphony of flavors that is the world of cooking, few instruments resonate as deeply as the wok. This unassuming yet mighty vessel has, for centuries, been the secret weapon of chefs and home cooks alike. It is with great joy and anticipation that I invite you to embark on a culinary journey through the pages of this cookbook, where the wok takes center stage, and its sizzling wonders unfold.

The art of wok cooking is not just a collection of recipes; it is a celebration of tradition, a fusion of cultures, and a testament to the ingenuity of generations past. In the heart of kitchens across continents, the wok has played a starring role, transforming raw ingredients into flavorful masterpieces with each toss and turn.

As we delve into the pages ahead, imagine the lively markets of Asia, where the aroma of spices and the rhythmic clang of the wok create a sensory symphony. These recipes draw inspiration from the rich tapestry of global cuisines, embracing the diverse techniques and ingredients that make wok cooking a culinary adventure like no other.

The wok, in its simplicity, is a storyteller. It whispers tales of faraway lands and brings to life the essence of different cultures. Through its sizzle and stir, we connect with the roots of culinary traditions that have stood resilient against the ever-changing tides of time.

This cookbook is an invitation to explore the vast possibilities that unfold when you wield the wok in your kitchen. Whether you are a seasoned chef or a novice home cook, these recipes are crafted to inspire and empower you to create delicious, memorable meals. The wok becomes more than a cooking tool; it becomes a companion in your culinary escapades.

In a world where time seems to move faster than ever, the wok grounds us. It encourages us to slow down, to appreciate the process, and to savor the journey as much as the destination. It is a reminder that the act of cooking is an art, a labor of love that extends beyond the confines of the kitchen.

So, as you embark on this flavorful expedition, I encourage you to embrace the sizzle, relish the aromas, and savor the moments of creation. May these wok wonders bring joy to your table, spark creativity in your kitchen, and become a source of shared delight for you and your loved ones.

Here's to the sizzle, the stir, and the infinite possibilities that await in the world of wok cooking.

Happy cooking!

Chapter 1

Unveiling the Wok's Culinary Canvas

Origins of the Wok

Ancient Beginnings: Tracing the Wok's Roots The story of the wok begins in ancient China, where its origins are intertwined with the rich culinary heritage of the Han Dynasty (206 BCE–220 CE). Initially crafted from cast iron, these early woks featured a deep, rounded shape with a small base—ideal for cooking over traditional wood-fired stoves. The design facilitated efficient heat distribution, ensuring that ingredients were cooked swiftly and evenly.

As we delve further into the annals of Chinese history, we encounter the wok's early use in street food stalls and bustling markets. Its versatility quickly made it a staple in Chinese kitchens, adapting to various cooking methods, from stir-frying to deep-frying and steaming. The wok became a vessel for culinary experimentation, allowing cooks to showcase their creativity while preserving the integrity of flavors.

EVOLUTION ACROSS CULTURES: HOW THE WOK TRAVELED THE GLOBE

While the wok's origins lie in China, its journey transcended geographical boundaries, weaving itself into the fabric of diverse culinary traditions. The Silk Road, the ancient network of trade routes connecting East and West, played a pivotal role in the wok's global migration. As merchants and travelers traversed these routes, they carried not only goods but also culinary practices.
In Southeast Asia, the wok became a cornerstone of Thai, Vietnamese, and Malaysian cuisines. Its adaptability to high-heat cooking methods made it an indispensable tool for creating the bold and vibrant flavors characteristic of these regions. The sizzling sounds of a wok echoed in street markets, where hawkers skillfully tossed ingredients, creating aromatic masterpieces that delighted passersby.

The wok's influence extended far beyond Asia, making its mark in the kitchens of Europe and the Americas. In the 20th century, with the surge of interest in international cuisines, the wok gained popularity in Western kitchens. Chinese stir-fry became a household favorite, and soon, innovative chefs began incorporating the wok into non-traditional recipes, leading to a fusion of flavors that reflected the evolving global palate.

Today, the wok stands as a symbol of cultural exchange and culinary fusion. Its adaptability has allowed it to seamlessly integrate into kitchens worldwide, from the traditional wok ranges of Chinese restaurants to the modern stovetops of home cooks seeking a taste of authenticity. The wok's journey from ancient China to kitchens across the globe is a testament to its enduring appeal and the universal language of delicious food.

The Anatomy of a Wok

DESIGN AND CONSTRUCTION: UNDERSTANDING THE WOK'S UNIQUE SHAPE

At first glance, the wok's design appears deceptively simple, yet its shape is a carefully crafted masterpiece that serves both form and function. The hallmark of the wok is its concave shape—a shallow, wide basin with high, sloping sides. This configuration allows for a large surface area at the bottom, ideal for high-heat cooking techniques like stir-frying.

The high, sloping sides of the wok serve a crucial purpose in facilitating the tossing and stirring of ingredients with ease. This unique design enables the cook to manipulate the food swiftly over the intense heat at the center of the wok, ensuring that each morsel is perfectly cooked while retaining its distinct texture and flavor. The wok's versatility is further enhanced by its ability to accommodate different cooking methods, from deep-frying to steaming, making it a multifaceted kitchen workhorse.

Beyond its shape, the construction of the wok is equally important. Traditional woks are often made from materials such as carbon steel or cast iron, prized for their durability and ability to retain and distribute heat efficiently. More modern iterations may include materials like stainless steel or non-stick coatings, catering to contemporary cooking preferences without compromising on the wok's essential characteristics.

MATERIALS MATTER: EXPLORING THE VARIOUS WOK MATERIALS

Carbon Steel: The Traditional Workhorse The majority of traditional woks are crafted from carbon steel, known for its excellent heat conductivity and durability. Carbon steel woks respond quickly to changes in temperature, allowing for precise control during cooking. Additionally, they develop a natural non-stick patina over time, enhancing their cooking performance with continued use.

Cast Iron: The Sturdy Heirloom Cast iron woks boast exceptional heat retention, making them ideal for slow cooking and deep-frying. While they are heavier than their carbon steel counterparts, cast iron woks are favored for their longevity and the ability to create a perfect sear on ingredients.

Proper seasoning is key to maintaining and enhancing the performance of cast iron woks.

Stainless Steel: The Modern Alternative Stainless steel woks have gained popularity for their durability, resistance to rust, and sleek appearance. While they may not offer the same rapid heat conductivity as carbon steel or cast iron, stainless steel woks are valued for their low maintenance and suitability for induction cooktops.

Non-Stick Coatings: Convenience in the Kitchen Non-stick woks, often made from materials like PTFE or ceramic coatings, appeal to cooks seeking convenience and ease of cleaning. While not traditional, these woks provide a hassle-free cooking experience and are suitable for those prioritizing health-conscious, oil-free cooking.

THE ART OF THE SEAR: STIR-FRYING MASTERY

Stir-frying is the heartbeat of wok cookery, an ancient technique that has become synonymous with the wok itself. The magic unfolds in the sizzle as ingredients dance across the searing heat, creating a symphony of flavors and textures. The key to stir-frying mastery lies in the combination of high heat, quick cooking, and the constant movement of ingredients.

The high, sloping sides of the wok facilitate the toss-and-turn method, allowing food to cook rapidly while maintaining its natural crispness and vibrancy. A successful stir-fry achieves the delicate balance of caramelization, with ingredients kissed by the flames, resulting in a harmonious blend of savory, sweet, and umami notes. Whether it's a classic vegetable stir-fry or a protein-packed delight, stir-frying in the wok unlocks a world of possibilities for culinary creativity.

BEYOND STIR-FRYING: DEEP FRYING, STEAMING, AND MORE

While stir-frying may be the wok's most celebrated technique, its versatility extends far beyond the quick and lively dance of ingredients in the searing heat. The wok serves as a versatile stage for a variety of cooking methods, each contributing to the symphony of flavors in its own unique way.

Deep Frying: Golden Crispiness with a Wok Twist The wok's deep, wide basin is an ideal vessel for deep frying, a technique that achieves a perfect balance of crispiness and succulence. Whether it's golden spring rolls, crispy tempura, or crunchy chicken, the wok's high sides and efficient heat distribution make it a reliable partner in the pursuit of deep-fried perfection.

Steaming: Gentle Elevation of Flavors Elevating the wok to new heights, steaming emerges as a technique that embraces the gentle side of cooking. with the addition of a bamboo or metal steamer insert, the wok transforms into a vessel for preparing delicate dumplings, fluffy buns, and perfectly steamed fish. The gentle, enveloping heat of the wok ensures that flavors meld harmoniously without sacrificing nutritional value.

Braising and Boiling: Infusing Richness into Ingredients The wok's versatility extends to braising and boiling, techniques that infuse ingredients with rich, savory flavors. The wide surface area of the wok allows for even distribution of liquid, creating stews, soups, and braised dishes that simmer to perfection. The result is tender meat, flavorful broths, and a culinary experience that resonates with warmth and depth.

From the vibrant wok dance of stir-frying to the gentle embrace of steaming, the wok proves its versatility as a culinary maestro, orchestrating a symphony of flavors that transcends culinary boundaries.

Chapter 2

The Basics and Sauces

Basic Chinese Brown Sauce

Prep time: 5 minutes | Cook time: 10 minutes | Serves ⅔

- ½ cup beef broth
- 1 tablespoon soy sauce
- 1 tablespoon oyster sauce
- 1 tablespoon Chinese rice wine or dry sherry
- 1 teaspoon granulated sugar
- 1 teaspoon sesame oil
- ¼ teaspoon black pepper
- 2 teaspoons cornstarch

1. In a bowl, whisk together the beef broth, soy sauce, oyster sauce, rice wine, sugar, sesame oil, and pepper until combined.
2. Whisk in the cornstarch. Either use the sauce immediately or store in a sealed container in the refrigerator until ready to use. (Use the sauce within 3 or 4 days.) Stir the sauce before adding it to the stir-fry to bring up any cornstarch that has settled on the bottom.

Sesame Sauce

Prep time: 5 minutes | Cook time: 10 minutes | Serves ½

- 4 tablespoons chicken broth
- 2 tablespoons red wine vinegar or Chinese red rice vinegar
- 2 tablespoons soy sauce
- 2 tablespoons sesame oil
- ½ tablespoon granulated sugar
- ¼ teaspoon chili paste
- 2 garlic cloves, finely minced
- 2 teaspoons cornstarch

1. Combine the chicken broth, vinegar, soy sauce, sesame oil, sugar, chili paste, and garlic in a bowl.
2. Whisk in the cornstarch. Either use the sauce immediately or store in a sealed container in the refrigerator until needed. (Use the sauce within 3 or 4 days.) Stir the sauce before adding to the stir-fry to bring up any cornstarch that has settled on the bottom.

Thai Chicken Stock

Prep time: 15 minutes | Cook time: 25 minutes | Makes 2 quarts (1.9 l)

- 1 chicken carcass or whole chicken cut into 8 pieces
- cold water to cover
- 8 cups (1.9 l) water
- 3" (8-cm) piece thinly sliced galangal
- 2 stalks lemongrass, thick lower portion only, pounded
- 2–3 kaffir lime leaves
- 2 cloves garlic, peeled
- 1 large shallot, peeled and sliced
- 2 thai chilies, pounded with the knife

1. Place a cut-up whole chicken or boned carcass in an 8-quart (7.6-L) stockpot and cover with cold water. Bring the bones to a boil and simmer for 5 minutes. Remove the bones and rinse and wash under running cold water until the sediment and scum have washed away.
2. Add the galangal, lemongrass, kaffir lime leaves, garlic cloves, shallots and chilies to the pot and allow to simmer. Skim off the foam and fat often, and continue to simmer for about 1½ hours.
3. Skim off any additional fat and strain the stock through a cheesecloth-lined sieve. If not using this stock immediately, you can hold it for about a week in the fridge or freeze it for 6 months.

Chinese Chicken Soup Stock

Prep time: 15 minutes | Cook time: 25 minutes | Makes 1 gallon (3.8 l)

- 1 whole chicken, cut into 8 pieces (skin off)
- 1 lb (450 g) pork neck bones
- 4 qt (3.8 l) cold water
- 2" (5-cm) piece ginger
- 1 clove garlic, pounded
- 2 scallions, chopped into thirds
- ½ tsp white peppercorns
- 2 tbsp (30 ml) oyster sauce
- salt to taste

1. Bring 3 quarts (2.9 L) water to a boil in a large stockpot. Add the chicken pieces and pork neck bones, and boil for about 3 to 5 minutes. This will bring out blood and scum. Pour off the water and rinse the chicken.
2. Place the chicken and pork back into the pot. Add 4 quarts (3.8 L) of cold water and all the ingredients except salt. Bring the water to a boil and cover it. Reduce the heat to a medium simmer and leave the lid slightly cracked. Simmer it for about 2 to 4 hours, skimming the scum occasionally. Season with salt to taste.
3. Let the stock cool, then strain out and discard the solids. Stock can be refrigerated for up to 4 or 5 days.

Sriracha Mayo and Wasabi Mayo

**Prep time: 15 minutes | Cook time: 25 minutes |
Makes scant ¾ cup (170 g) of each**

Sriracha Mayo:

- ½ cup (113 g) mayonnaise
- 2 tbsp (30 ml) sriracha chili sauce
- 1 tsp sesame oil

Wasabi Mayo:

- 2 tbsp (10 g) wasabi powder (horseradish powder)
- 2 tbsp (30 ml) water
- ½ cup (113 g) mayonnaise

1. Stir each set of ingredients together until thoroughly mixed.

Simple Stir-Fry Sauce

**Prep time: 5 minutes | Cook time: 5 minutes |
Serves ½**

- 3 tablespoons soy sauce
- 3 tablespoons water
- 1 tablespoon oyster sauce
- 2 teaspoons red wine vinegar
- 2 teaspoons granulated sugar
- 1 teaspoon garlic salt
- ¼ teaspoon black pepper

1. Combine all the ingredients in a small bowl.
2. Use as called for in a recipe, or store in a sealed container in the refrigerator until ready to use.

Korean-Inspired Marinade

Prep time: 6 minutes | Cook time: 10 minutes | Serves ½

- 2 tablespoons orange juice
- 2 tablespoons soy sauce
- 1 tablespoon honey
- 1 tablespoon brown sugar
- 1 tablespoon rice wine or sherry
- 1 tablespoon sesame oil
- ¼ teaspoon black pepper
- ½ Asian pear, finely grated
- 1 scallion, sliced
- 1 teaspoon toasted sesame seeds

1. Prepare the beef for stir-frying, cutting according to the recipe directions.
2. In a large bowl, whisk together the marinade ingredients. Place the beef in the bowl, ensuring that it has been evenly coated. Cover the bowl and allow the beef to marinate in the refrigerator for at least 1 hour.

Peanut Sauce

Prep time: 15 minutes | Cook time: 25 minutes | Makes about 2½ cups

- 2 tbsp (30 ml) vegetable oil
- 1 tbsp (16 g) red curry paste, or more to taste
- 2 cups (490 ml) coconut milk
- 2 tbsp (30 g) chunky peanut butter, or more to taste
- 2 tbsp (30 ml) fish sauce
- ½ tsp rice vinegar
- 2 tbsp (30 g) sugar, or more to taste

1. Heat the oil in a small saucepan over high heat. When hot, stir-fry the curry paste for about a minute or until very fragrant and thick.
2. Stir in the coconut milk and bring it to a boil; cook for 2 minutes while constantly stirring. Be careful not to let it boil over. about 2 to 3 minutes.
3. Reduce the heat to a simmer and add the fish sauce, rice vinegar and sugar. An oily film will rise to the top; skim it off if you wish.

Chapter 3

Egg and Tofu

Vegetarian Tofu Stir-Fry

Prep time: 10 minutes | Cook time: 10 minutes | Serves 2

- 1/4 cup frozen edamame without shell (green soybeans)
- 1/8 teaspoon salt
- 1 tablespoon of olive oil
- 1 clove of chopped garlic
- 1 cup of sliced yellow pepper
- 1/2 cup sliced yellow onion
- 1/2 cup bean sprouts
- 1 tablespoon of tamari soy sauce
- 2 cups of cooked pasta
- 1 tablespoon of sesame oil
- 1 teaspoon of roasted sesame seeds

1. Mix edamame and salt in a microwave-safe bowl; Cover and cook in the microwave for 1 minute. Heat the olive oil in a large wok over medium heat; Add garlic and cook until fragrant and sizzle, about 1 minute.
2. Add paprika and onion; cook and stir until they start to brown, about 2 minutes. Add bean sprouts and soy sauce; cook and stir until the soy sauce starts to evaporate, about 1 minute.
3. Add Edam, cooked noodles, sesame oil and sesame seeds; stir until the soy sauce starts to evaporate, about 30 seconds.

Fried Tofu with Tomato Sauce

Prep time: 6 minutes | Cook time: 10 minutes | Serves 4

- 1 tablespoon vegetable oil
- 1 tablespoon minced garlic
- 1/4 cup diced shallots
- 4 Roma tomatoes, seeded and roughly diced
- 2 scallions, thinly sliced
- 1 red jalapeño, thinly sliced
- 1/4 cup ketchup
- 1 tablespoon fish sauce
- 4 cups fried tofu, cubed
- 1/2 teaspoon black pepper
- 1/4 cup cups chopped cilantro
- 2 cups steamed white rice

1. In a wok, heat oil over medium heat and add the garlic and shallots. Cook for about 2 minutes.
2. Add tomatoes, scallions, and jalapeño and cook for an additional 2–3 minutes until softened.
3. Stir in ketchup and fish sauce. Lower the heat and simmer for about 5 minutes.
4. Toss in fried tofu and coat evenly. Season with black pepper and garnish with fresh cilantro. Serve with rice.

Chinese Chives Eggs Stir-Fry

Prep time: 10 minutes | Cook time: 7 minutes | Serves 6

- 5 large eggs
- 1/8 teaspoon sugar
- ½ teaspoon salt
- 1 teaspoon Shaoxing wine
- ¼ teaspoon ground white pepper
- ¼ teaspoon sesame oil
- 4 teaspoons water
- 2 cups Chinese chives, chopped
- 4 tablespoons vegetable oil

1. Beat eggs with sugar, salt, wine, white pepper, water, chives, and sesame oil in a bowl.
2. Set up a wok on medium heat and add vegetable oil to heat.
3. Pour the egg-wine mixture and stir-fry for 5–7 minutes until eggs are set.
4. Serve warm.

Chinese Tomato and Egg

Prep time: 15 minutes | Cook time: 15 minutes | Serves 6

- 225 g boneless pork loin, cut into thin strips
- 2 tablespoons of soy sauce
- 1 tablespoon of brandy1 teaspoon of white sugar
- 1 tablespoon of cornstarch
- 4 eggs
- 8 large tomatoes, cut into pieces
- 1 teaspoon of white sugar
- 2 bunches of chopped green onions

1. Mix the pork, soy sauce, brandy, 1 teaspoon sugar and corn starch in a bowl, then cover with cling film and marinate in the refrigerator for 4 to 6 hours.
2. Heat half of the oil in a wok over medium to high heat. Take out of the wok and set aside. Heat the rest of the vegetable oil in the wok over high heat.
3. Stir in the tomatoes and the remaining 1 teaspoon of sugar.Puree the tomatoes until the mixture resembles a chunky soup.

Chinese Steamed Eggs

Prep time: 5 minutes | Cook time: 20 minutes | Serves 4

- 3 medium eggs
- 2 teaspoons sea salt
- 1 cup water
- Soy sauce
- Sesame oil
- 1 scallion, finely chopped

1. In a large bowl, beat the eggs. Pour the eggs through a sieve into a steam-proof dish. Add the sea salt to the dish, and whisk it into the eggs.
2. In your wok over high heat, bring the water to a boil. Place a steamer rack or colander with legs in the wok. Carefully place the dish with the eggs in the wok, and cover the dish with a heat-proof plate. Turn the heat to low, and steam the eggs for 15 minutes.
3. Carefully remove the dish. Serve the eggs with soy sauce and sesame oil and garnished with a chopped scallion.

Salt and Black Pepper Tofu

Prep time: 10 minutes | Cook time: 5 minutes | Serves 6

Tofu Brine:

- 14 ounces firm tofu, sliced
- ¼ teaspoon garlic powder
- ½ teaspoon onion powder
- ½ teaspoon salt
- 1 teaspoon sugar
- 1 ¼ cups warm water
- ½ teaspoon sesame oil
- 1 teaspoon shaoxing wine

Tofu Seasoning:

- ¾ teaspoon salt
- ¾ teaspoon ground white pepper
- ¼ teaspoon ground sichuan peppercorn
- ¼ teaspoon sand ginger powder
- 2 tablespoons all-purpose flour
- 2 tablespoons cornstarch

1. Mix tofu with all of its brine ingredients in a bowl and cover to marinate for 2 hours.
2. Whisk flour with cornstarch, peppercorn, white pepper, salt, and ginger powder in a bowl.
3. To cook the tofu, heat oil in a Cantonese wok.

Red Miso Soup with Tofu

Prep time: 15 minutes | Cook time: 25 minutes | Serves 4

- 3–4 cups (710–946 ml) dashi stock
- ¼ cup (50 g) fresh shiitake mushrooms, sliced very thin
- ¼ cup (50g) dried wakame seaweed, rinsed and chopped
- ¼–½ cup (50–100 g) red miso
- 4 oz (100 g) block soft tofu in water, cut into small cubes
- 2–3 scallions, finely sliced on a bias

1. Heat the stock in a medium wok over medium heat until just under a simmer.
2. Add the mushrooms and seaweed and allow to cook for about 5 minutes or until the mushrooms have softened.
3. Submerge a small sieve into the wok until the rim is just above the stock. Add the miso into the sieve and use a wooden spoon to work the miso through into the soup. This will prevent lumps from forming. Stir well and taste the soup; if not salty enough, add additional miso.
4. Add the tofu and scallions; allow to cook for about a minute. The scallions will perfume the soup and give it an earthy sweetness.

Savory Steamed Egg Custard

Prep time: 10 minutes | Cook time: 10 minutes | Serves 4

- 4 large eggs, at room temperature
- 1¾ cups low-sodium chicken broth or filtered water
- 2 teaspoons Shaoxing rice wine
- ½ teaspoon kosher salt
- 2 scallions, green part only, thinly sliced
- 4 teaspoons sesame oil

1. In a large bowl, whisk the eggs. Add the broth and rice wine and whisk to combine. with a paring knife, pop any bubbles on the surface of the egg mixture. Cover the ramekins with aluminum foil.
2. Rinse a bamboo steamer basket and its lid under cold water and place it in the wok. Place the ramekins in the steamer basket. Cover with the lid.
3. Bring the water to a boil, then reduce the heat to a low simmer. Steam over low heat for about 10 minutes or until the eggs are just set.
4. Carefully remove the ramekins from the steamer and garnish each custard with some scallions and a few drops of sesame oil. Serve immediately.

Tofu Salad with Tangy Sesame Dressing

Prep time: 15 minutes | Cook time: 25 minutes | Serves 4

Dressing:

- 6 tbsp (48 g) japanese sesame powder, or toasted sesame seeds
- ⅔ cup (160 g) mayonnaise
- ¼ cup (60 ml) rice vinegar
- 1 tbsp (8 g) minced ginger root
- 3 tbsp (45 ml) water
- 2 tsp (10 g) salt
- 3 tbsp (40 g) sugar

Salad:

- 1 (14-oz [400-g]) carton medium tofu
- 1 small ripe plum or roma tomato, sliced
- 1 small japanese cucumber, sliced
- ½ cup (40 g) thinly sliced nori
- ¼ cup (37 g) furikake topping

For the Dressing:

1. Combine all the dressing ingredients in a blender and purée until smooth, about 30 seconds. Set the dressing aside in the refrigerator until ready to use.

For the Salad:

2. Drain the tofu and pat it dry with paper towels. Cut the tofu in half lengthwise, making large planks, then place those planks in the middle of a serving plate.

Broccoli and Tofu Stir Fry

Prep time: 5 minutes | Cook time: 25 minutes | Serves 4

- 1 tbsp peanut oil
- 4 cloves of chopped garlic
- 1 red pepper, deseeded and cut into strips
- 2 crowns of broccoli, cut into florets
- 1/3 cup chicken broth
- 3 tbsp soy sauce
- 1 tbsp dry sherry
- 2 tbsp corn starch
- 8 ounces extra diced firm tofu
- 2 tbsp cashew pieces

1. Heat the peanut oil in a large pan or wok over high heat. Fry and stir the garlic for a few seconds until it begins to turn brown.
2. Cook and stir the broccoli and bell peppers for 5 minutes until the bell peppers turn soft and brown - Stir cornstarch, chicken broth, sherry and soy sauce together until the cornstarch dissolves.
3. Pour the sauce into the pan and bring to the boil. Cook the tofu for a minute, stirring until hot.
4. Place the cashew pieces on top and serve.

Gingered Tofu

Prep time: 10 minutes | Cook time: 25 minutes | Serves 6

- 21 ounces firm tofu, cut into cubes
- 2 tablespoons oil
- 4 ginger slices
- 1 tablespoon shaoxing wine
- 2 tablespoons chinese black vinegar
- 3 tablespoons light soy sauce
- 4 tablespoons sugar
- 5 tablespoons water

1. Sauté ginger with oil in a Cantonese wok for 30 seconds.
2. Stir in tofu, and sauté for 10 minutes until it turns golden.
3. Add wine, black vinegar, soy sauce, water, and sugar.
4. Cover and cook for 15 minutes over medium low heat.
5. Serve warm.

Mapo Tofu

Prep time: 9 minutes | Cook time: 30 minutes | Serves 4

- $1/2$ pound ground pork
- 1 tablespoon soy sauce
- 1 teaspoon granulated sugar
- $1/4$ teaspoon black pepper
- 3 teaspoons cornstarch, divided
- 4 teaspoons water plus 2 tablespoons, divided
- $3/4$ pound firm tofu, drained and cut into $1/2$ cubes

1. In a large bowl, combine the ground pork with the soy sauce, sugar, black pepper, and 1 teaspoon cornstarch. Marinate the pork for 15 minutes.
2. In a small bowl, dissolve 2 teaspoons cornstarch into 4 teaspoons water. Set aside.
3. Rinse the black beans under cold running water for 10 minutes, drain, and chop. Place the black beans in a bowl with the garlic and mash with a fork. Stir in 2 tablespoons water.

Chapter 4

Poultry

Thai-Style Cashew Chicken

Prep time: 5 minutes | Cook time: 12 minutes | Serves 4

1 pound boneless, skinless chicken breasts
3/4 cup unsalted cashews
2 tablespoons vegetable or peanut oil
6–10 small Thai red chili peppers
1 1/2 tablespoons oyster sauce
1 medium white onion, chopped
2 scallions, finely chopped
1/4 cup chicken broth
1 1/2 tablespoons fish sauce
1 tablespoon palm sugar

1. Cut the chicken into bite-sized cubes.
2. Roast the cashews in a heavy skillet over medium heat, shaking the pan continuously so that the nuts do not burn. Roast until the cashews are browned (about 5 minutes). Remove the cashews from the pan to cool.
3. Turn up the heat to medium high and add the oil. When the oil is hot, add the red chili peppers. Cook for 1 minute or until they begin to darken. Use a slotted spoon to remove the chilies.
4. Add the chicken to the wok and stir-fry until it is nearly cooked through—about 3–4 minutes. Stir in the oyster sauce while the chicken is stir-frying.
5. Add the onion and scallions. Stir-fry for 2 minutes, until the onion begins to soften.

Sweet-and-Sour Chicken

Prep time: 5 minutes | Cook time: 30 minutes | Serves 4

1 1/2 pounds boneless, skinless chicken breasts
1 tablespoon soy sauce
1 tablespoon oyster sauce
2 teaspoons cornstarch
1/4 cup pineapple juice
2 tablespoons vinegar
2 tablespoons brown sugar
2 tablespoons olive oil
3 slices fresh ginger
3 scallions, cut into thirds

1. Cut the chicken into bite-sized cubes. Place the chicken cubes in a bowl and add the soy sauce, oyster sauce, and cornstarch. Marinate the chicken for 20 minutes.
2. In a small bowl, combine the pineapple juice, vinegar, and brown sugar. Set aside.
3. Heat a wok or skillet on medium-high heat until it is nearly smoking. Add the oil. When the oil is hot, add the ginger slices. Let the ginger slices cook for 2–3 minutes, until they are browned. Remove the ginger.
4. Add the chicken cubes. Stir-fry, stirring and tossing the chicken for 3–4 minutes until it changes color and is nearly cooked through.

Chicken and Snow Peas Stir-Fry

Prep time: 15 minutes | Cook time: 15 minutes | Serves 6

- 1 cup of chicken broth
- 3 tablespoons of soy sauce
- 1 tablespoon of cornstarch
- 1 tablespoon of ground ginger
- 2 tablespoons of vegetable oil
- 4 large skin and bone halves of chicken breast, cut into cubes
- 2 cloves of garlic, chopped
- 1 1/2 cups sliced fresh mushrooms
- 2 (225 g) cans of sliced and drained water chestnuts
- 3 cups of sugar peas
- 1 tablespoon of sesame seeds

1. Whisk the chicken stock, cornstarch, soy sauce and ginger in a small bowl and set aside. In a large pan or wok, heat the oil and fry the chicken and garlic for 8-10 minutes until the chicken is cooked through.
2. Add the water chestnuts, mushrooms and the reserved chicken broth mixture while stirring. Cook for 3-5 minutes until the sauce starts to thicken.
3. Add the sugar snap peas to the pan while stirring and cook for 3-5 minutes until tender.
4. Place on a plate or platter, sprinkle with sesame seeds and serve.

Chicken Wings with Black Bean Sauce

Prep time: 25 minutes | Cook time: 40 minutes | Serves 4

- 900 gr. chicken wings
- 1/2 cup of chicken broth with reduced sodium content
- 2 teaspoons of soy sauce
- 2 teaspoons of cornstarch
- 1 teaspoon of sugar
- 2 tablespoons of peanut or vegetable oil
- 1 tablespoon of drained fermented black beans from china
- 1/8 teaspoon dried hot red pepper flakes
- a well-seasoned 35 cm flat-bottom wok with a lid

1. Pat the chicken wings dry, cut off the tips with a large, Mix the broth, soy sauce, cornstarch and sugar in a small bowl until the sugar is dissolved.
2. Woke over high heat until a bead of water evaporates immediately. pinch of salt and stir-fry, allowing the wings to rest for 5 to 10 seconds between stirs, until golden brown, 8 to 10 minutes.
3. Add black beans, garlic, ginger and red pepper flakes then add to the wok and brush the wings while stirring.
4. Bring the sauce to a boil, then reduce the heat and simmer covered, stirring occasionally, until the wings are tender, about 15 minutes.

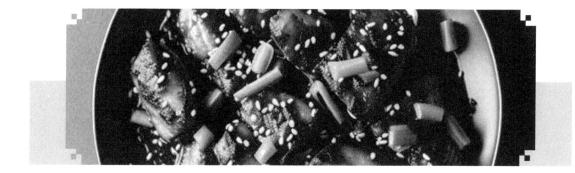

Ginger Cashew Chicken

Prep time: 25 minutes | Cook time: 15 minutes | Serves 6

- 1 1/2 cups of chicken broth
- 1/2 cup soy sauce
- 1 tablespoon of cornstarch
- 3/4 teaspoon ground ginger
- 3/4 teaspoon brown sugar
- 1/4 cup cornstarch
- 1 1/2 teaspoons of ground ginger
- 1/4 teaspoon curry powder
- 3 green onions, chopped
- 1 pepper, chopped
- 1 teaspoon sesame seeds
- 1/2 cup cashew nuts

1. Mix the chicken broth, soy sauce, 1 tablespoon cornstarch, 3/4 teaspoon ground ginger and brown sugar in a bowl. Mix 1/4 cup of cornstarch, 1 1/2 teaspoons of ground ginger and curry powder in a large, sealable plastic bag and shake.
2. Heat the olive oil and sesame oil in a wok or large pan over high heat. Cook the chicken in the hot oil and stir until golden brown (3 to 5 minutes).
3. Scatter sesame seeds over the dish and bring to the boil; Cook for 3 to 5 minutes, until the sauce is thick. Remove from stove. Add cashew nuts and toss to serve.

Sesame Chicken

Prep time: 8 minutes | Cook time: 40 minutes | Serves 2

- 1/2 pound boneless, skinless chicken breast
- 1 tablespoon soy sauce
- 1 egg white
- 3 teaspoons cornstarch, divided
- 1/3 cup plus 4 teaspoons water, divided
- 1 tablespoon vinegar
- 1 tablespoon granulated sugar
- 1/2 teaspoon chili paste
- 2 tablespoons vegetable or peanut oil, divided
- 1 thin slice ginger
- 2 cloves garlic, chopped
- 1 scallion, finely chopped
- 1 tablespoon toasted sesame seeds

1. Cut the chicken into bite-sized cubes and place in a bowl. Combine with the soy sauce, egg white, and 1 teaspoon cornstarch. Marinate the chicken in the refrigerator for 30 minutes.
2. In a medium bowl, combine 1/3 cup water, vinegar, sugar, and the chili paste.
3. In a separate bowl, dissolve 2 teaspoons cornstarch in 4 teaspoons water. Set aside.
4. Heat a wok or skillet over medium-high heat until it is nearly smoking. Add 1 1/2 tablespoons oil. When the oil is hot, add the ginger. Let brown for 2–3 minutes, then remove from the pan.

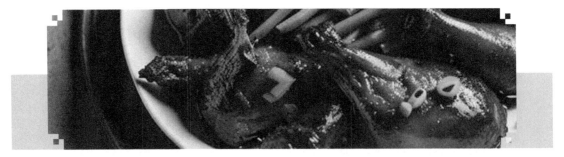

Chinese Chicken Salad

Prep time: 15 minutes | Cook time: 25 minutes | Makes 2½ cups (120 ml) of dressing

Dressing:

- 5 green onions (2″ [5-cm]) white parts only, thinly sliced
- 1 tbsp (15 g) chinese dry mustard, made into a paste by stirring in 1 tbsp (15 ml) water
- ⅓ cup (85 g) japanese pickled ginger, packed
- ½ cup (120 ml) lime juice
- 1 tbsp (9 g) roughly chopped garlic
- 2 tbsp (16 g) roughly chopped ginger root
- 2 cups (480 ml) peanut oil

Salad:

- 1 cup (240 g) canned tangerine segments, drained
- 5 cups (500 g) napa cabbage
- 2 carrots, peeled and cut into thin strips
- 3 cups (711 ml) oil
- 5 wonton wrappers
- 2 tbsp (12 g) toasted sesame seeds

For the Dressing:

1. Combine all the ingredients except the peanut oil in a blender. Blend them thoroughly for about 10 seconds, until no one item is recognizable.
2. with the blender running, slowly drizzle in the peanut oil until the dressing is smooth and even. You can use immediately or store in an air-tight container for a week.

For the Salad:

1. In a large salad bowl, toss the tangerines, cabbage, carrots, radicchio, greens and chicken.
2. Heat the oil in a small saucepan over medium-high heat. Cut the wonton skins into ¼-inch (6-mm) wide strips. When the oil reaches 365°F (185°C), fry until the strips are golden brown, about 30 seconds on each side. Drain the wonton strips on a paper towel and allow to cool. You'll need about 2 cups (90 g) of wonton strips. Toss them with the salad.

Chinese Braised Duck Legs

Prep time: 10 minutes | Cook time: 45 minutes | Serves 4

- 4 duck legs
- ¼ cup Shaoxing wine
- 2 cups chicken stock
- 2 tablespoons soy sauce
- 2 tablespoons oyster sauce
- ½ teaspoon sesame oil
- 3 ginger slices
- 3 garlic cloves, sliced
- 12 scallions, cut into 2-inch pieces

1. Sauté ginger and garlic with sesame oil in a large wok for 1 minute.
2. Stir in chicken stock, wine, soy sauce, oyster sauce, and white pepper.
3. Mix well and cook this mixture to a simmer.

Peking Duck

Prep time: 10 minutes | Cook time: 20 minutes | Serves 4

Duck:

- 4 boneless duck breasts
- ¼ teaspoon salt
- 1 teaspoon light soy sauce
- 1 teaspoon shaoxing wine
- 1/8 teaspoon five spice powder
- 1 tablespoon oil

Fixings:

- 1 cucumber, julienned
- ½ cup cantaloupe, julienned
- 2 scallions, julienned
- 3 garlic cloves, finely minced
- 3 tablespoons hoisin sauce

1. Mix wine, five-spice powder, soy sauce, and salt in a bowl.
2. Soak the duck breasts in the marinade for 20 minutes for marination.
3. Sear the marinated duck breast in a Mandarin wok greased with oil over medium heat for 10 minutes per side until golden-brown.
4. Mix cucumber with cantaloupe, scallions, garlic, and hoisin sauce in a bowl.
5. Serve the duck breast with cucumber mixture.
6. Enjoy.

Kung Pao Chicken

Prep time: 6 minutes | Cook time: 28 minutes | Serves 4

$3/4$ pound boneless, skinless chicken breasts
5 teaspoons rice vinegar, divided
2 teaspoons soy sauce
$1^1/2$ teaspoons cornstarch
$1^1/2$ tablespoons dark soy sauce
1 tablespoon water
1 teaspoon granulated sugar
2 tablespoons vegetable or peanut oil
3 dried chili peppers
2 slices ginger
1 tablespoon chopped garlic
1 cup unsalted peanuts

1. Cut the chicken into 1 cubes. Place the chicken cubes in a bowl and add 3 Marinate the chicken for 20 minutes.
2. In a small bowl, combine the dark soy sauce, water, sugar, and 2 teaspoons rice vinegar. Set aside.
3. Heat a wok or skillet over medium-high heat until it is almost smoking. Add the oil. Let brown for 2–3 minutes, and then remove.
4. Add the chicken. Let brown briefly, then stir-fry, stirring and tossing the chicken until it turns white and is nearly cooked—about 3–4 minutes. Remove the chicken from the pan.

Chapter 5

Beef, Pork, and Lamb

Beef Stir-Fry with Vegetables

Prep time: 5 minutes | Cook time: 20 minutes | Serves 4

- ¾ pound boneless sirloin
- Oyster-Flavored Marinade for Beef
- 3 tablespoons vegetable or peanut oil, divided
- 2 thin slices ginger
- 1 teaspoon salt
- 1 medium red bell pepper, seeded and cut into strips lengthwise
- ½ teaspoon black pepper

1. Cut the beef across the grain into thin strips approximately 2 long. Place the beef in a bowl and add the marinade. Marinate the beef for 15 minutes.
2. Heat a wok or skillet on medium-high heat until it is nearly smoking. When the oil is hot, add the ginger and let brown for 2–3 minutes. Remove the pieces of ginger.
3. Clean out the wok and add 1 tablespoon oil. When the oil is hot, add salt and the bamboo shoots. Stir-fry briefly for about 1 minute, splashing the bamboo shoots with the rice wine or sherry.

Chinese Fried Ribs

Prep time: 10 minutes | Cook time: 7 minutes | Serves 6

- 2 pounds pork ribs, cut into 1-inch nuggets
- 1 large piece red fermented bean curd
- ½ teaspoon ground white pepper
- 1 teaspoon sesame oil
- 1 teaspoon five spice powder
- 2 tablespoons shaoxing wine
- 1 tablespoon soy sauce
- 1 tablespoon maple syrup
- ½ teaspoon garlic powder
- ½ teaspoon onion powder
- ½ teaspoon baking soda
- ¼ cup cornstarch
- 3 cups canola oil

1. Mix bean curd, white pepper, sesame oil, spice powder, wine, soy sauce, maple syrup, garlic powder, onion powder, baking soda, and cornstarch in a bowl.
2. Stir in pork ribs and mix well to coat.
3. Cover the pork and marinate for 1 hour in the refrigerator.
4. Add 3 cups canola oil in a deep wok and heat up to 350ºF.
5. Deep fry the pork chunks for 7 minutes until golden-brown.
6. Serve warm.

Pork and Bamboo Shoots

Prep time: 15 minutes | Cook time: 15 minutes | Serves 2

- 1 tbsp peanut oil
- 1 (400 g) can of thinly sliced bamboo shoots
- 2 tbsp peanut oil
- 2 cloves of chopped garlic
- 1 fresh red chili pepper (deseeded and chopped)
- 1/2 teaspoon of crushed red pepper flakes
- 3.0 ounces minced pork
- 1 teaspoon of shaoxing rice wine
- salt to taste
- 2 teaspoons rice vinegar
- 2 teaspoons of soy sauce
- 3 tablespoons of chicken broth
- 3 green onions (thinly sliced)
- 1 teaspoon sesame oil

1. Put the wok on medium heat and heat 1 tablespoon of peanut oil. Take the bamboo shoots off the stove and set them aside.
2. Turn the heat on high and add the rest of the peanut oil. Fry red pepper flakes, garlic and red chili until they are fragrant. Add the pork and fry until cooked through.
3. Add the green onions and remove the mixture from the heat. Serve with sesame oil on top.

Sesame Beef Stir-Fry

Prep time: 25 minutes | Cook time: 15 minutes | Serves 6

- 1/2 cup soy sauce
- 1/2 cup white sugar
- 1/3 cup rice wine vinegar
- 1/3 cup chopped garlic
- 1 tablespoon of sesame seeds
- 1 pound round steak, thinly sliced
- 1/4 cup peanut oil
- 2 cups of sliced asparagus
- 1 tablespoon corn starch (optional)
- 1 tablespoon of water (optional)
- 1 tablespoon of sesame seeds

1. Whisk the soy sauce, sugar, rice wine vinegar, garlic and 1 tablespoon of sesame seeds in a bowl; Fill in a resealable plastic bag. Add beef, coat with marinade, squeeze out excess air and seal the bag.
2. Marinate the beef in the refrigerator overnight. Heat peanut oil in a wok or large pan over medium-high heat; Boil and stir the beef and marinade until the beef is well browned, about 5 minutes.
3. Mix cornstarch and water in a small bowl for 2 to 3 minutes; stir into the beef and fry until the sauce has thickened, about 3 minutes. Sprinkle with the remaining 1 tablespoon of sesame seeds.

Asian Pork Burgers

Prep time: 9 minutes | Cook time: 10 minutes |
Serves 2

- 1 cup shredded purple cabbage
- ½ cup shredded carrots
- ½ cup Chili Ponzu Marinade
- ½ pound lean ground pork
- ½ tablespoon minced garlic
- 1 teaspoon minced ginger
- 1 teaspoon minced lemongrass
- 1 tablespoon fish sauce
- 2 scallions, minced
- 2 tablespoons vegetable oil
- 2 tablespoons Wasabi Aioli
- 2 hamburger buns, toasted

1. To make the cabbage slaw, toss the cabbage and carrots in a medium bowl with the marinade. Cover and refrigerate for 1 hour.
2. Heat the vegetable oil in a wok over medium heat Add both pork patties, side by side. Cook the patties for 2 minutes on each side until the pork is golden brown and cooked through. Remove from wok.
3. Assemble the burgers by spreading the Wasabi Aioli inside both sides of the toasted buns. Layer with a pork patty and a heaping mound of the cabbage slaw. Serve immediately.

Sichuan Pork Stir-Fry

Prep time: 30 minutes | Cook time: 15 minutes |
Serves 2

- 6 leaves of stem lettuce, cut into pieces
- 1 pinch of salt
- 2 teaspoons of water
- 1 teaspoon corn starch
- 7.94 ounces lean pork, cut into cubes
- 1 teaspoon rice wine (sake)
- 1/4 teaspoon salt
- 2 teaspoons of chili bean sauce
- 3 diced spring onions
- 2 cloves of sliced garlic
- 1 piece of sliced fresh ginger

1. Mix a pinch of salt and stem salad in a bowl. In a separate small bowl, mix the cornstarch and water until a smooth paste is formed. Put 1/2 of the cornstarch paste in a large bowl.
2. Add the marinated pork with the marinade and stir-fry for 3 to 4 minutes, or until the pork is browned. Add the chili bean sauce and the pickled chili peppers and fry for about 1 minute or until the oil turns red.
3. Add the garlic, ginger and spring onions and stir-fry for about 1 minute or until they are fragrant. Add the sauce and stir well for about 3 minutes until it thickens.

Zucchini with Lamb Stir Fry

Prep time: 10 minutes | Cook time: 15 minutes | Serves 4

- 1 pound ground lamb
- 4 tablespoons of soy sauce
- 1 tablespoon of chopped fresh ginger
- 1 tablespoon of chopped garlic
- 2 teaspoons plus 2 tablespoons of cornstarch
- 1 cup of canned low-salt chicken stock
- 2 tablespoons of fresh lemon juice
- 2 teaspoons of garlic and chili sauce
- 3 tablespoons of vegetable oil
- 2 tablespoons of oriental sesame oil
- 3 large cloves of peeled garlic
- 1.3 pounds zucchini (cut into strips)

1. Mix the lamb, 2 tablespoons soy sauce, ginger, minced garlic and 2 teaspoons cornstarch in a large bowl. Mix the broth, lemon juice, chili sauce and the remaining 2 tablespoons of soy sauce and 2 tablespoons of cornstarch in a small bowl.
2. Heat both oils in a wok or in a Dutch oven over high heat. Add 3 cloves of garlic; Cook for about 2 minutes until golden brown.
3. Discard the garlic. Add the zucchini and onion; Fry while stirring until they are crispy and tender, about 3 minutes.
4. Season with salt and pepper. Serve with rice.

Stir-Fry Beef and Potatoes

Prep time: 8 minutes | Cook time: 20 minutes | Serves 6

- 1 pound rib eye steak, thinly sliced
- 1 tablespoon minced garlic
- 1½ teaspoons cornstarch
- ½ teaspoon black pepper
- 2 cups plus 3 tablespoons vegetable oil, divided
- 2 large Russet potatoes, peeled and cut into ¼-wide strips
- 1 small yellow onion, quartered
- 2 tablespoons Maggi Seasoning or low-sodium soy sauce
- ¼ cup cilantro leaves

1. In a bowl, mix together the beef, garlic, cornstarch, black pepper, and 1 tablespoon vegetable oil. Set aside.
2. Heat 2 cups oil in a heavy pot until it
3. Heat 2 tablespoons oil in a large wok over medium heat. Add onion and mushrooms and cook until both have softened but not browned, approximately 3–4 minutes.
4. Add the tomatoes and cook for an additional 2 minutes.
5. To serve, place the potatoes in a layer on a rimmed plate. Pour beef stir-fry over the top and garnish with cilantro. Serve immediately.

Chapter 6

Fish and Seafood

Simple Stir-Fried Fish

Prep time: 5 minutes | Cook time: 20 minutes | Serves 4

- 1 pound fish fillets, such as cod or pollock
- 1/2 teaspoon salt
- 1/4 teaspoon ground black pepper
- 1 egg white
- 2 tablespoons Chinese rice wine or dry sherry, divided
- 2 teaspoons cornstarch
- 2 tablespoons vegetable or peanut oil
- 2 thin slices ginger
- 1 scallion, finely chopped
- 1 tablespoon soy sauce
- 1 teaspoon Asian sesame oil

1. Cut the fish fillets into 1 1/2"–2" squares that are about 1/2" thick. Place the fish cubes in a large bowl and add the salt, black pepper, egg white, 1 tablespoon Chinese rice wine or sherry, and the cornstarch. Marinate the fish for 15 minutes.
2. Heat a wok or skillet over medium-high heat until it is nearly smoking. Add the oil. When the oil is hot, add the ginger and scallion. Stir-fry for 10 seconds.
3. Splash the fish cubes with the remaining 1 tablespoon rice wine or sherry and the soy sauce. Let the fish cook for another minute, remove it from the heat, and stir in the sesame oil. Serve hot.

Salt and Pepper Shrimp

Prep time: 5 minutes | Cook time: 10 minutes | Serves 4

- 1 pound medium to large shrimp, shells on
- 2 tablespoons cornstarch
- 3/4 teaspoon kosher or sea salt
- 3/4 teaspoon freshly ground black pepper
- 2 cups vegetable or peanut oil
- 1 teaspoon minced ginger
- 1/2 teaspoon minced garlic
- 1 shallot, chopped
- 1 scallion, finely chopped

1. Rinse the shrimp under cold running water and pat dry with paper towels. Dredge the shrimp in the cornstarch. Place the dredged shrimp on a plate next to the stove.
2. In a small bowl, combine the salt and pepper.
3. Heat a wok or skillet over medium-high heat and add the oil. When the oil is hot, carefully add the shrimp. Cook until the shrimp turns pink and the edges begin to curl (about 1 minute). Remove the shrimp and drain in a colander or on paper towels.
4. Stir in the salt and pepper mixture from step 2. Stir in the scallion. Stir-fry for 1 minute to combine the ingredients. Serve hot.

Spicy Shrimp with Peanuts

Prep time: 5 minutes | Cook time: 20 minutes | Serves 2

- 1 pound large shrimp, peeled and deveined
- 1 teaspoon kosher salt
- 1 tablespoon red wine vinegar
- 1 tablespoon soy sauce
- 1 tablespoon water
- 1 teaspoon granulated sugar
- 2 tablespoons vegetable or peanut oil
- 2 teaspoons minced ginger
- 2 scallions, finely chopped
- 6–8 small red chilies, seeded and chopped
- 1/2 cup peanuts

1. Rinse the shrimp under cold running water. Place the shrimp in a bowl and soak in warm water with the salt for 15 minutes. Remove. Pat the shrimp dry with paper towels.
2. In a small bowl, combine the red wine vinegar, soy sauce, water, and sugar. Set aside.
3. Add the shrimp. Stir-fry the shrimp for 1 minute or until they turn pink, then add the vinegar sauce.
4. Stir in the peanuts. Cook for another 2 minutes to heat through, then serve hot.

Basic Stir-Fried Scallops

Prep time: 5 minutes | Cook time: 10 minutes | Serves 4

- 1 pound sea scallops
- 1/2 teaspoon kosher salt
- 1 tablespoon cornstarch
- 2 tablespoons vegetable or peanut oil
- 1 teaspoon minced ginger
- 2 teaspoons soy sauce
- 1/4 teaspoon chili paste
- 1/2 teaspoon granulated sugar
- 3 green scallions, chopped

1. Rinse the scallops in cold running water and pat dry with paper towels. Place the scallops in a bowl and toss with the salt and the cornstarch.
2. Heat a wok or skillet over medium-high heat until it is nearly smoking. Add the oil. When the oil is hot, add the ginger. Stir-fry for 10 seconds.
3. Add the scallops and stir-fry for 1 minute, then splash with the soy sauce. Stir in the chili paste, sugar, and scallions. Continue stir-frying until the scallops are white but not too firm (total stir-frying time should be 2–3 minutes). Serve hot.

Chinese Take-Out Prawns

Prep time: 15 minutes | Cook time: 10 minutes | Serves 4

- 2 tablespoons of rapeseed oil
- 10 cloves of garlic (chopped)
- 1 teaspoon of chopped fresh ginger root
- 1 can of chopped water chestnuts (drained)
- 1 cup of sugar peas
- 1 cup of small white mushrooms
- 1 teaspoon of crushed red pepper flakes
- 1 pound peeled and deveined jumbo prawns
- 1/2 cup of chicken broth
- 1 tablespoon rice vinegar
- 2 tablespoons of fish sauce
- 2 tablespoons of dry sherry
- 1 tablespoon cornstarch
- 1 tablespoon of water

1. Heat a large pan or wok with oil until the oil is very hot. Add the ginger and garlic and fry in the hot oil for 30 seconds or until fragrant.
2. In a small bowl, mix rice vinegar, dry sherry, chicken broth and fish sauce together.
3. Add the sauce mixture to the shrimp mixture and cook and stir for a few seconds to mix well.
4. Mix the water and cornstarch together and add it to the wok. Cook and stir the mixture for 2 minutes or until the sauce is thick.

Korean Spicy Stir-Fry Squid

Prep time: 7 minutes | Cook time: 10 minutes | Serves 4

- 1 pound large squid tubes
- 2 tablespoons gojuchang paste
- 2 tablespoons soy sauce
- 1 teaspoon sesame oil
- 1/2 tablespoon honey
- 1/2 tablespoon rice wine vinegar
- 2 tablespoons vegetable oil
- 1 teaspoon finely minced ginger
- 2 scallions, cut into 1" pieces
- 1/2 teaspoon ground black pepper

1. Cut the squid tubes in half lengthwise. Score the squid tubes in a crisscross pattern by holding the knife at a 45-degree angle and making a series of cuts, and then holding the knife at a 120-degree angle and making a second series of cuts. Cut the scored squid into 1" squares.
2. In a small bowl, whisk together the gojuchang, soy sauce, sesame oil, honey, and vinegar. Set aside.
3. Add in the bell pepper and yellow onion and cook for an additional 2–3 minutes.
4. Add the squid, scallions, and several spoonfuls of the gojuchang sauce. Cook for an additional 1–2 minutes or until the squid is opaque. Season with black pepper and serve immediately.

Corn Salad with Crabs

Prep time: 20 minutes | Cook time: 5 minutes | Serves 6

- 4 ears of corn, kernels cut from the cob
- 2 leeks, only the white parts (thinly sliced)
- 2 cloves of chopped garlic
- 2 avocados, peeled, pitted and diced into pieces
- 1/2 lemon, squeezed
- 5 tbsp vegetable oil
- 1 tbsp rice vinegar vegetable oil
- 1 tablespoon rice vinegar
- 1 tablespoon of chopped fresh basil
- 1 teaspoon of salt
- 1/2 teaspoon of chopped fresh tarragon
- 2 cans of lumpy crab meat (drained and flaked)

1. Put the corn kernels in a sieve to separate the small pieces; put in a bowl. In a separate bowl, stir together the lemon juice and diced avocado so they don't turn brown.
2. Heat vegetable oil in a pan over high heat; Add corn mixture. Cook for 4-8 minutes, stirring, until the corn is evenly brown.
3. Mix the tarragon, corn mixture, salt, avocado, basil and rice vinegar in a serving bowl.
4. Put the crab meat on top.

Coconut Mango Salad with Shrimp

Prep time: 15 minutes | Cook time: 25 minutes | Serves 4

- 1 tbsp (15 ml) vegetable oil
- ½ lb (240 g) medium shrimp, sliced in half lengthwise
- 2 shallots, thinly sliced
- 2 cloves garlic, finely chopped
- ½ cup (95 g) brown sugar or palm sugar
- 3 cups (720 g) matchstick-cut green mango
- 1 cup (75 g) toasted coconut chips
- ½ red onion, very thinly sliced
- 3 scallions, cut on the bias
- ¼ cup (35 g) cashew nuts, roasted

1. Heat a medium skillet on medium and add oil. When you see a wisp of white smoke, add the shrimp and lightly sauté them for about 1 minute, then reduce the heat to low. Add the shallots, garlic and Thai chilies and cook them for an additional minute, until the shrimp are just cooked through.
2. Turn off the heat. Stir in the lime juice, fish sauce and sugar. When ready to serve, arrange the mango, coconut and red onion in the serving bowl. Toss to combine, and garnish with scallions and cashews.

Wok-Smoked Salmon

Prep time: 20 minutes | Cook time: 20 minutes | Serves 4

- ½ cup soy sauce
- ¼ cup Shaoxing rice wine
- 1 tablespoon minced fresh ginger
- 1 teaspoon honey
- 1 pound fresh salmon fillet, cleaned and patted dry
- 4 tablespoons brown sugar
- ⅓ cup uncooked long-grain rice
- ¼ cup black tea leaves, such as oolong
- 2 star anise pods
- 1 teaspoon cornstarch, mixed with 4 teaspoons cold water

1. In a large bowl, make a marinade by mixing together the soy sauce, rice wine, ginger, and honey. Cut the salmon fillet into 2-inch pieces, and add the pieces to the bowl; toss to coat with the marinade. Let the salmon marinate for 15 minutes.
2. Pour the marinade into a small saucepan and bring it to a boil. Remove it from the heat, and slowly add the cornstarch mixture to the marinade, stirring constantly until the sauce thickens.
3. Remove the smoked salmon from the wok, and place on a serving dish. Drizzle it with the sauce and serve with rice.

Steamed Cantonese-Style Sea Bass

Prep time: 10 minutes | Cook time: 15 minutes | Serves 4

- 1.3 pounds whole sea bass (or striped sea bass) with head and tail, scaled and without gills
- 1/4 cup plus 2 tablespoons of white wine
- 3 cloves of garlic, roughly chopped (approx. 2 tablespoons)
- 4 tablespoons of chopped green onions, including greens
- 2 tablespoons of finely chopped fresh ginger
- 2 teaspoons of sugar
- 1/4 cup olive oil 3 tablespoons soy sauce

1. Choose a round or oval plate that is big enough to hold the fish but fits in the top of a steamer. This can be a traditional Chinese bamboo or metal steamer, or a western steamer for clams.
2. Place the fish on the plate and place the plate on top of the steamer. Cover the plate with boiling water and steam covered for 10 to 15 minutes. Mix 2 tablespoons of wine, garlic, spring onions, ginger and sugar in a small bowl and prepare the sauce in the meantime.
3. Heat the oil in a wok or saucepan and add the sauce base when it is hot. Pour the soy sauce over the sea bass first then pour the cooked sauce over the fish.

Chapter 7

Vegetables

Korean Vegetables with Gochujang

Prep time: 15 minutes | Cook time: 6 minutes |
  Serves 4

- 2 tablespoons cooking oil
- 1 tablespoon crushed, chopped ginger
- 2 garlic cloves, crushed and chopped
- 1 medium onion, cut into 1-inch pieces
- 4 ounces shiitake mushrooms, sliced
- 2 cups sugar snap or snow pea pods
- 1 red bell pepper, cut into 1-inch pieces
- 2 heads baby bok choy, leaves separated
- 2 tablespoons gochujang
- ½ cup kimchi
- 2 tablespoons soy sauce

1. In a wok over high heat, heat the cooking oil until it shimmers.
2. Add the ginger, garlic, and onion and stir-fry for 1 minute.
3. Add the mushrooms and stir-fry for 1 minute.
4. Add the pea pods and stir-fry for 1 minute.
5. Serve over steamed jasmine rice.

Stir-Fry Cabbage

Prep time: 10 minutes | Cook time: 5 minutes |
  Serves 4

- 1 tablespoon of vegetable oil
- 2 cloves of garlic, chopped
- 0.9 pounds of chopped cabbage
- 1 tablespoon of soy sauce
- 1 tablespoon of Chinese cooking wine (Shaoxing wine)

1. Heat the vegetable oil in a wok or large pan over medium heat. Stir in the garlic and cook for a few seconds until it begins to brown.
2. Stir in the cabbage until it is covered in oil; cover the wok and cook for 1 minute.
3. Add the soy sauce and cook for another minute and stir. Turn the heat on high and stir in the Chinese cooking wine.
4. Cook and stir until the cabbage is tender, about 2 more minutes.

Thai Vegetables with Basil

Prep time: 15 minutes | Cook time: 6 minutes | Serves 4

- 2 tablespoons red Thai curry paste
- 2 tablespoons fish sauce
- 1 teaspoon hot sesame oil
- Juice of 1 lime
- 3 tablespoons brown sugar
- 1 tablespoon cornstarch
- 2 tablespoons cooking oil
- 2 cups sugar snap or snow pea pods
- 1 red bell pepper, cut into 1-inch pieces
- 2 cups basil leaves
- 1 cup fresh bean sprouts
- ½ cup chopped cilantro

1. In a small bowl, whisk together the curry paste, fish sauce, sesame oil, lime juice, brown sugar, and cornstarch. Set aside.
2. In a wok over high heat, heat the cooking oil until it shimmers.
3. Add the onion and stir-fry for 1 minute.
4. Add the pea pods and stir-fry for 1 minute.
5. Add the basil and toss for 30 seconds until it wilts.
6. Serve over rice or noodles, topped with the bean sprouts and cilantro.

Dry-Fried Green Beans

Prep time: 5 minutes | Cook time: 8 minutes | Serves 4

- ¼ cup peanut or vegetable oil
- 1 pound string beans, trimmed and completely dry
- 1 clove garlic, crushed
- 2 tablespoons oyster sauce
- 1 teaspoon Shaoxing rice wine
- 3 scallions, thinly sliced

1. Place your wok over high heat. When it is hot, add the peanut oil. Add the string beans to the wok, and cook them until they are crinkly and blistered, tossing them continuously for about 5 minutes. Remove the beans from the wok.
2. Keeping the wok over high heat, add the crushed garlic, oyster sauce, rice wine, and scallions to the wok and stir-fry until fragrant, about 30 seconds. Return the green beans to the wok, and toss them in the sauce until they are coated. Stir-fry the beans for 1 minute. Serve hot.

Chilled Sesame Broccoli Salad

Prep time: 15 minutes | Cook time: 25 minutes | Serves 6-8

- ¼ cup (60 ml) unseasoned rice wine vinegar
- 2 tbsp (30 ml) sesame oil
- ¼ cup (80 g) honey
- 3 tbsp (45 ml) soy sauce
- 2 lb (900 g) broccoli florets
- 2 tbsp (12 g) sesame seeds, toasted

1. Combine the rice wine vinegar, sesame oil, honey and soy sauce to make the dressing; set aside. May be prepped ahead for up to a week.
2. Bring about 2 quarts (1.8 L) of water to a rolling boil in a 4-quart (4.7-L) saucepan. Salt the water generously. Blanch the broccoli about 2 minutes, until it's al dente and bright green. Shock in a large bowl of ice water for about 3 minutes. Drain in a colander and reserve.
3. To serve, toss the chilled broccoli in a large bowl with the dressing until it's coated well. Sprinkle the broccoli with sesame seeds and serve.

Bok Choy with Garlic

Prep time: 10 minutes | Cook time: 5 minutes | Serves 4

- 1½ pounds baby bok choy
- 1½ tablespoons peanut or vegetable oil
- 1 or 2 garlic cloves, minced
- ¼ teaspoon ground ginger
- 3 tablespoons vegetable broth
- Sea salt
- ½ teaspoon toasted sesame oil

1. Trim the root ends of the baby bok choy. Wash and thoroughly drain the leaves.
2. Heat your wok to medium-high; add the peanut oil and swirl to coat the wok. Add the garlic and ginger, and cook them for 30 seconds to 1 minute. Do not let them burn. When the spices become fragrant, add the bok choy leaves. Stir-fry everything together until well combined.
3. Add the vegetable broth to the wok. Cover the wok and cook for about 1 minute. Remove the cover from the wok, and turn off the heat. Season the bok choy with the sea salt, drizzle it with the sesame oil, and toss to coat. Serve immediately.

Stir-Fried Bean Sprouts

Prep time: 5 minutes | Cook time: 5 minutes |Serves 4 to 6

- 1 tablespoon peanut oil
- 1 garlic clove, minced
- ½ carrot, julienned
- 4 cups fresh mung bean sprouts, rinsed
- 2 teaspoons soy sauce
- ¼ cup chopped garlic chives
- pinch ground white pepper

1. In a wok over high heat, heat the peanut oil.
2. Add the garlic and stir-fry for just a few seconds until aromatic.
3. Add the carrot and stir-fry for 2 or 3 seconds.
4. Toss the bean sprouts into the wok, followed by the soy sauce. Stir well for a few seconds then turn off the heat.
5. Add the garlic chives and pepper at the last minute, and transfer to a serving bowl.

Spinach with Bamboo Shoots

Prep time: 10 minutes | Cook time: 10 minutes | Serves 6

- 1 pound fresh spinach
- 1/2 cup of peanut, vegetable, or corn oil
- 1/4 cup finely chopped bamboo shoots
- 1 1/2 teaspoons of salt
- 2 teaspoons of sugar

1. Wash the spinach leaves thoroughly under running cold water, drain well and heat the oil in a wok or pan.
2. Cook the bamboo shoots in the oil over a medium-high flame for about 45 seconds, stirring constantly, add the spinach and stir until they are wilted, add salt and sugar and cook for about 1 1/2 to 2 minutes longer while stirring.
3. Place on a hot plate, but do not add the liquid from the pan.

Vietnamese Vegetables with Fish Sauce

Prep time: 15 minutes | Cook time: 5 minutes | Serves 4

- 1 tablespoon cooking oil
- 3 scallions, minced
- 1 medium red onion, diced
- 2 garlic cloves, crushed and chopped
- 1 cup sliced mushrooms
- 1 chile, cut crosswise, into ⅛- to ¼-inch rings
- 2 cups sugar snap or snow pea pods
- 1 cup ¼-inch sliced Napa cabbage
- 2 tablespoons fish sauce
- 2 tablespoons rice wine
- ¼ teaspoon ground white pepper
- ½ cup coarsely chopped cilantro, parsley, dill, or mint

1. In a wok over high heat, heat the cooking oil until it shimmers.
2. Add the scallions, onion, and garlic and stir-fry for 30 seconds.
3. Add the mushrooms and stir-fry for 30 seconds.
4. Add the chile and stir-fry for 30 seconds.
5. Toss the fish sauce, rice wine, and white pepper with the vegetables for 30 seconds.
6. Serve over steamed rice or noodles, topped with the fresh herbs of your choice.

Indian Five-Spice Vegetables

Prep time: 15 minutes | Cook time: 6 minutes | Serves 4

- 2 tablespoons cooking oil
- 2 garlic cloves, crushed and chopped
- 1 medium carrot, roll-cut into ½-inch pieces
- 1 medium onion, cut into 1-inch pieces
- 2 cups sugar snap pea pods
- 1 medium poblano pepper, cut into 1-inch pieces
- 1 red bell pepper, cut into 1-inch pieces
- 4 scallions, cut into 1-inch slices
- ¼ teaspoon ground cumin
- ¼ teaspoon ground coriander
- ¼ teaspoon ground cloves
- ¼ teaspoon ground turmeric
- ¼ teaspoon ground fennel
- 1 teaspoon hot sesame oil

1. In a wok over high heat, heat the cooking oil until it shimmers.
2. Add the garlic and carrot and stir-fry for 1 minute.
3. Add the onion and stir-fry for 1 minute.
4. Add the pea pods and stir-fry for 1 minute.
5. Add the cumin, coriander, cloves, turmeric, fennel, and sesame oil and stir-fry for 30 seconds.
6. Serve over steamed basmati rice.

Chapter 8

Noodle, Rice Dishes and Soups

Basic Stir-Fry Noodles

Prep time: 5 minutes | Cook time: 10 minutes | Serves 4

- 2 quarts water
- 1 teaspoon salt
- ½ pound linguine or Chinese egg noodles
- 2 teaspoons vegetable, peanut, or sesame oil

1. In a large wok, bring the water to a boil with the salt. Add the noodles and cook for 8–10 minutes or until they are firm but tender.
2. Drain the noodles thoroughly. Stir in the oil.
3. Use the noodles as called for in a stir-fry recipe. Adding noodles to the stir-fry allows them to soak up the sauce.

Egg Drop Soup

Prep time: 10 minutes | Cook time: 10 minutes | Serves 4 to 6

- 8½ cups vegetable broth, divided
- 1 ounce dried, sliced shiitake or tree ear mushrooms
- ¼ cup cornstarch
- 4 large eggs, beaten
- 4 scallions, both white and green parts, cut into ¼-inch pieces

1. In the wok, combine 8 cups of broth and the mushrooms. Bring to a boil.
2. In a small bowl, create a slurry with ¼ cup of cornstarch and the remaining ½ cup of broth.
3. Garnish with the scallions, bruising them by squeezing them while dropping them into the broth. Serve immediately.

Winter Melon and Pork Soup

Prep time: 15 minutes | Cook time: 20 minutes | Serves 4 to 6

- 8 cups broth (meat, seafood, or vegetable)
- 1 (15-ounce) can straw mushrooms, drained and rinsed
- 8 ounces ground pork
- 1 tablespoon chopped fresh ginger
- 3 garlic cloves, crushed and chopped
- 2 tablespoons soy sauce
- 2 tablespoons shaoxing cooking wine
- 2 cups winter melon, peeled, cored, and cut into bite-size pieces
- 4 scallions, both white and green parts, cut into ¼-inch pieces

1. In the wok, bring the broth and mushrooms to a simmer over medium heat.
2. In a bowl, combine the pork, ginger, garlic, soy sauce, and wine.
3. Roll the pork mixture into ½-inch meatballs and add them to the simmering broth.
4. Add the winter melon to the broth and cook for 10 minutes, until softened.
5. Add the scallions and serve.

Hot and Sour Soup

Prep time: 20 minutes | Cook time: 15 minutes | Serves 4

- 4 ounces boneless pork loin, cut into ¼-inch-thick strips
- 1 tablespoon dark soy sauce
- 4 dried shiitake mushrooms
- 8 dried tree ear mushrooms
- 1½ tablespoons cornstarch
- ¼ cup unseasoned rice vinegar
- 2 tablespoons soy sauce
- 2 teaspoons sugar
- 1 teaspoon chili oil (optional)
- 1 teaspoon ground white pepper
- 2 tablespoons cooking oil
- 1 large egg, lightly beaten
- 2 scallions, both white and green parts, thinly sliced, for garnish

1. In a bowl, toss the pork and dark soy sauce to coat. Set aside.
2. Stir the cornstarch into the reserved mushroom liquid until the cornstarch has dissolved. Stir in the vinegar, soy sauce, sugar, chili oil (if using), and white pepper. Once the sugar has dissolved, set aside.

Chicken Lo Mein

Prep time: 7 minutes | Cook time: 20 minutes | Serves 4

- 1½ teaspoons salt, divided
- ½ pound fresh egg noodles or linguine
- 1 cup chicken broth
- 2 tablespoons soy sauce
- ¼ pound mushrooms, thinly sliced
- 6 ounces snow peas, trimmed
- 1 medium red bell pepper, thinly sliced
- ¼ teaspoon black pepper

1. In a large pot, bring 2 quarts water to a boil with 1 teaspoon salt. If using linguine, cook for 8–10 minutes. Drain the cooked pasta.
2. Heat a wok or skillet over medium-high heat until it is nearly smoking. When the oil is hot, add the crushed garlic and stir-fry for 10 seconds.
3. Return the chicken to the pan. Stir-fry for 2 more minutes or until everything is heated through. Season with the black pepper and remaining salt. Serve hot.

Rice Fried with Bacon

Prep time: 5 minutes | Cook time: 30 minutes | Serves 4

- ½ pound bacon, cut into small pieces
- 2 tablespoons of soy sauce
- 2 chopped green onions
- 1/4 teaspoon sea salt
- 2 cups of steamed white rice

1. Put the bacon in a wok or a large pan and cook over medium heat for about 5 minutes, stirring occasionally, until it starts to brown.
2. Pour the soy sauce on top and scrape up the brown pieces from the bottom of the wok. Add green onions and salt; Cook for 30 seconds to 1 minute until wilted.
3. Add rice; Cook for 3 to 4 minutes, stirring frequently, until the soy sauce is heated through.

Vegetable Wonton Soup

Prep time: 30 minutes | Cook time: 10 minutes | Serves 4 to 6

- 8 cups vegetable broth
- 1 ounce dried tree ear mushrooms
- 8 ounces extra-firm tofu, drained and crumbled
- 2 garlic cloves, crushed and chopped
- 2 tablespoons chopped, fresh ginger
- 2 tablespoons hoisin sauce
- 6 scallions, both white and green parts, minced and divided
- 1 (12-ounce) package square wonton wrappers
- 2 cups sliced bok choy

1. In the wok, bring the broth to a simmer, then add the dried mushrooms.
2. In a food processor or on a cutting board, combine and chop together the crumbled tofu, garlic, ginger, hoisin sauce, and 2 minced scallions.
3. After 1 minute of boiling, put the sliced bok choy in the soup and boil for 1 minute until bright green.
4. Add the remaining scallions to the soup and serve.

Kimchi Fried Rice

Prep time: 15 minutes | Cook time: 25 minutes | Serves 4

- 2 tbsp (30 ml) cooking oil
- 1 tbsp (15 ml) sesame oil
- 2 eggs, lightly beaten
- 3 cloves garlic, coarsely chopped
- 3 tbsp (45 ml) soy sauce
- 1 tbsp (15 g) sugar
- 3 green onions, sliced on the bias
- 1 tsp white pepper

1. In a large wok, heat the oils until a wisp of white smoke appears. Add the eggs and lightly scramble them until just set, about 1 to 2 minutes.
2. Add the salt, soy sauce and sugar. Continue to fold the rice for about 1 to 2 minutes. Don't be afraid to scrape the rice stuck to the bottom of the pan. Cook it for about 1 more minute until the rice absorbs the sauces and is slightly crisp on the edges.
3. Fold in the green onions and white pepper, cook for an additional minute. Serve immediately.

Coconut Chicken Soup

Prep time: 15 minutes | Cook time: 25 minutes | Makes 1 quart (946 ml)

- 3 cups (720 ml) Thai Chicken Stock
- 6 oz (180 g) boneless, skinless chicken breasts, cut into 1" (2.5-cm) cubes
- 1 (15-oz [425-g]) can straw mushrooms, drained
- 1–3 thai chilies, split
- 5 tbsp (75 ml) fish sauce
- 1 (14-oz [414-ml]) can coconut milk (not light)
- 1½ cups (330 g) chopped cabbage
- kaffir (thai) lime leaves, for garnish
- cilantro leaves, for garnish

1. Bring the Thai Chicken Stock to a simmer over medium-high heat in a large wok.
2. Add the chicken, mushrooms and chilies and cook until the chicken is cooked through, about 4 minutes.
3. Stir in the fish sauce, lime juice, coconut milk and chili paste. Add the chopped cabbage and cook until just tender, about 1 minute.
4. Divide the soup among serving bowls and garnish each with 1 to 2 lime leaves and cilantro.

Singapore Noodles

Prep time: 7 minutes | Cook time: 20 minutes | Serves 4

- ½ pound flat rice stick noodles
- 1 pound small shrimp, shelled and deveined
- ½ cup chicken broth
- 2 tablespoons oyster sauce
- 1 teaspoon minced ginger
- 1 tablespoon Madras curry powder
- 6 ounces snow peas, trimmed
- 2 cups mung bean sprouts, rinsed and drained
- ½ teaspoon black pepper
- 1 scallion, chopped

1. Soak the rice noodles in warm water for 15 minutes or until they have softened. Drain the noodles.
2. Rinse the shrimp under cold running water and pat dry.
3. In a small bowl, combine the chicken broth, oyster sauce, and sugar. Set aside.
4. Stir in the black pepper. Stir-fry for 1 minute to heat everything through. Sprinkle with the chopped scallion. Serve hot.

Asian Shrimp Rice Bowl

Prep time: 15 minutes | Cook time: 1 hour 30 minutes | Serves 4

- 1/3 cup soy sauce
- 1/4 cup hoisin sauce
- 2 tablespoons of honey
- 1 tablespoon of chili paste
- 2 tablespoons of orange jam
- 225 g cooked shrimp
- 2 cups uncooked jasmine rice
- 1 sweet onion (cut into cubes)
- 4 cloves of chopped garlic
- 2 teaspoons of chopped fresh ginger root
- 1/4 teaspoon sesame oil
- 1 1/2 teaspoons of sesame seeds

1. Mix honey, orange jam, hoisin sauce, soy sauce and chili paste in a small bowl. Mix the prawns into the marinade and store in the refrigerator for 1 hour.
2. Heat a large pan or wok with oil. Cook red peppers, sugar snap peas, onions and orange-colored peppers in hot oil for 2-3 minutes and stir until the vegetables soften.
3. Mix in the ginger, garlic, sesame oil and the marinated prawns. Cook and stir for another 2-3 minutes until the prawns are fully heated.
4. Serve this dish with hot jasmine rice and a dash of sesame seeds.

Vegetable Chow Mein

Prep time: 6 minutes | Cook time: 10 minutes | Serves 2

- 1 teaspoon salt
- 1/2 pound fresh wheat noodles
- 1 cup unsalted cashews
- 2 tablespoons vegetable or peanut oil
- 1 teaspoon chopped fresh ginger
- 1/2 cup chopped yellow onion
- 1 small carrot, julienned
- 1 cup sliced mushrooms
- 1 cup snow peas
- 1 tablespoon soy sauce
- 1/3 cup Simple Stir-Fry Sauce
- 3/4 teaspoon granulated sugar

1. In a large pot, bring 2 quarts water to a boil with the salt. Add the noodles and cook for 1–2 minutes until they are firm but tender. Drain the noodles.
2. Roast the cashews in a heavy frying pan over medium heat, shaking the pan continuously so that the nuts do not burn. Roast until the cashews are browned (about 5 minutes). Remove the cashews from the pan to cool.
3. Add the noodles. Stir in the Simple Stir-Fry Sauce and bring to a boil.
4. Stir in the roasted cashews and the sugar. Stir-fry for 1 minute to heat everything through, and serve hot.

Chapter 9

Dumplings, Egg Rolls, and Dim Sum Favorites

Egg and Crab Lettuce Wraps

Prep time: 10 minutes | Cook time: 10 minutes |Serves 4 to 6

- 1 head lettuce
- 4 eggs, lightly beaten
- pinch salt
- pinch ground white pepper
- ½ teaspoon soy sauce
- 2 scallions, chopped
- 3 tablespoons peanut oil
- ½ cup diced water chestnuts
- 1 small onion, thinly sliced
- ¾ cup crabmeat
- ¼ cup basic sambal

1. Wash and separate the lettuce leaves. Chill the lettuce leaves in the refrigerator until just before serving.
2. Put the beaten eggs into a medium bowl. Add the salt, pepper, soy sauce, and scallions to the eggs. Stir gently just to combine.
3. In a wok over medium-high heat, heat the peanut oil.
4. Using a wok spatula, break up and scramble the egg.
5. Serve with the chilled lettuce leaves and sambal (if using).

Dim Sum Drum Dumpling

Prep time: 15 minutes | Cook time: 25 minutes | Makes about 8-10 dumplings

- 5 dried chinese black mushrooms
- ¾ lb (340 g) coarsely ground pork butt
- ½ lb (240 g) shrimp, peeled, deveined and coarsely chopped
- ½ tsp salt
- 2 tsp (10 g) sugar
- ½ tbsp (8 ml) peanut oil
- 1½ tbsp (22 ml) oyster sauce
- 1 tsp cornstarch
- 1 tbsp (15 ml) sesame oil

1. Reconstitute the mushrooms in hot water for 30 minutes. Rinse them, remove the stems and chop them into small dice.
2. In a large bowl, combine the remainder of the filling ingredients and mix until well combined. You may also use a mixer with a paddle attachment for this. Cover the mixture and let it rest in the refrigerator for at least an hour to overnight.
3. Steam the dumplings in a steamer basket on high for about 7 minutes or until cooked through.

Soup Dumplings

Prep time: 60 minutes | Cook time: 10 minutes | Makes 20 dumplings

- 1 cup hot tap water
- 1 teaspoon chicken, beef, or pork bouillon
- 1 (¼-ounce) package unflavored gelatin
- 4 ounces ground pork
- 2 scallions, both white and green parts, minced
- 1 teaspoon toasted sesame oil
- 20 (4-inch) round dumpling wrappers (if you use smaller wrappers, they will be harder to fold)
- 4 to 6 lettuce leaves

1. In a medium bowl, combine the hot tap water, bouillon, and gelatin, and mix until the gelatin dissolves. Put in the refrigerator or freezer until gelatinized.
2. In a large bowl, combine the pork, scallions, ginger, garlic, soy sauce, sugar, and sesame oil and mix well.
3. Transfer the gelatinized broth to the meat mixture and combine.
4. Place about 1 tablespoon of filling in the center of the wrapper, being careful not to get any filling on the outer ¼-inch edge of the wrapper.

Quick Steamed Pork Buns

Prep time: 20 minutes | Cook time: 20 minutes | Makes 8 buns (bao)

- 1 tablespoon cooking oil
- 1 pound pork belly or pork shoulder, diced into ¼-inch pieces
- ½ cup char siu sauce (such as lee kum kee or ah-so)
- 2 tablespoons brown sugar
- 1 (16-ounce) can buttermilk biscuits (8 large)

1. In the wok, heat the oil over high heat until it shimmers. Add the pork and stir-fry for 2 minutes.
2. Lower the heat to medium. Add the char siu sauce and brown sugar and cook for 5 minutes, until the pork is cooked through. Set aside to cool.
3. Roll out the biscuit dough into 4 circles.
4. Place 2 tablespoons of pork (charsiu) in the center of each circle of dough (bao).
5. Make a bun by pulling the perimeter of the circle toward the center, pinching and twisting the dough together, enclosing the filling completely.

Shrimp Dumplings

Prep time: 45 minutes | Cook time: 5 minutes | Makes 15 to 20 dumplings

For The Filling:

- 1 pound peeled and deveined shrimp, coarsely chopped
- ¼ cup diced water chestnuts
- 2 tablespoons cornstarch
- 2 tablespoons finely chopped fresh cilantro (optional)

For The Wrappers:

- 1¼ cups wheat starch
- 2 tablespoons tapioca flour
- 1¼ cups boiling water
- 1 teaspoon cooking oil

To Make The Filling:

1. In a large bowl, combine the shrimp, water chestnuts, cornstarch, sesame oil, soy sauce, and cilantro (if using). Mix well.
2. Marinate the mixture in the refrigerator for at least 30 minutes.

To Make The Wrappers:

1. In a large bowl, combine the wheat starch and tapioca flour.
2. Slowly pour the boiling water into the flour mixture, stirring continuously, until it starts to form a ball of dough.
3. Roll the dough out into a small pancake, about 3 inches in diameter.

Pork Egg Rolls

Prep time: 7 minutes | Cook time: 10 minutes | Serves 25

- 1 pound lean ground pork
- 1 tablespoon dark soy sauce
- 2 tablespoons oyster sauce
- 1 teaspoon minced garlic, divided
- 1 teaspoon minced ginger, divided
- 1 cup shredded carrots
- 2 scallions, finely chopped
- 1 teaspoon sesame oil
- 1 teaspoon black pepper
- 25 (6 × 6) egg roll wrappers
- 2 eggs, beaten
- 2 cups peanut or vegetable oil

1. In a large bowl, mix together the ground pork, soy sauce, oyster sauce, garlic, ginger, carrots, scallions, and sesame oil. Add the black pepper.
2. One at a time, place an eggroll wrapper on a flat surface with one of the points facing toward you. Press to seal, set aside, and continue with the remaining ingredients.
3. Heat the oil in a wok over high heat to 375°F. In batches, fry the egg rolls until golden brown, about 5–6 minutes. Remove the fried egg rolls to plates lined with paper towels to drain. Serve hot.

Deep-Fried Salmon and Miso Wontons

Prep time: 40 minutes | Cook time: 15 minutes | Makes 40 dumplings

- 1 (8-ounce) skinless salmon fillet
- 1 tablespoon white or yellow miso
- 2 fresh garlic cloves, crushed and chopped
- 1 teaspoon toasted sesame oil
- 1 tablespoon soy sauce
- 1 (12-ounce) package square wonton wrappers
- 2 cups oil, for deep-frying

1. In a food processor, combine and pulse the salmon, miso, garlic, sesame oil, and soy sauce.
2. To make the wontons, place a wonton wrapper on a work surface so it looks like a baseball diamond with you sitting behind home plate.
3. Fill a small bowl with water. Using a clean fingertip, paint around the baselines with the water.
4. Place a teaspoon of the filling in the center, where the pitcher's mound would be.
5. Deep-fry the wontons until golden brown color develops on both sides, flipping as needed.
6. Serve with your favorite dipping sauce.

San Xian Wontons

Prep time: 10 minutes | Cook time: 20 minutes | Serves 12

- 8 ounces shrimp; peeled, deveined, and chopped
- 8 ounces ground pork
- 8 ounces ground chicken
- 1 tablespoon ginger, minced
- ¼ cup scallion, chopped
- 2 tablespoons vegetable oil
- 2 tablespoons light soy sauce
- 1 tablespoon oyster sauce
- ½ tablespoon sesame oil
- ½ teaspoon ground white pepper
- ½ cup water
- 2 packages wonton wrappers

1. Sauté scallions and ginger with oil in a Mandarin wok until soft.
2. Stir in pork, chicken, shrimp, and rest of the ingredients (except the wrappers).
3. Sauté for about 8 minutes, then remove the filling from the heat.
4. Allow the filling to cool and spread the egg roll wrappers on the working surface.
5. Divide the pork-shrimp filling at the center of each wrapper.
6. Transfer the golden egg rolls to a plate lined with a paper towel.
7. Serve warm.

Japanese Gyoza Dumplings

Prep time: 10 minutes | Cook time: 30 minutes | Serves 12

- 5 cups Napa cabbage
- 8 ounces ground pork
- 1 garlic clove, smashed
- 1 ½ teaspoon fresh ginger, minced
- 1 scallion, chopped
- 2 tablespoons vegetable oil
- ½ teaspoon sesame oil
- 2 teaspoons soy sauce
- ¾ teaspoon sugar
- ½ teaspoon salt
- 1/8 teaspoons white pepper
- 24 store-bought gyoza wrappers

1. Sauté garlic, ginger, and scallions with oil in a Mandarin wok until soft.
2. Stir in cabbage, pork, and rest of the ingredients.
3. Sauté for about 7 minutes until veggies are cooked and soft.
4. Allow the filling to cool and spread the gyoza wrappers on the working surface.
5. Divide the pork filling at the center of each gyoza wrapper.
6. Sear the dumpling for 2 minutes until golden.
7. Serve warm.

Lion's Head Meatballs

Prep time: 20 minutes | Cook time: 20 minutes | Makes 4 large meatballs or 8 smaller "cubs"

- 1 pound ground pork
- 1 tablespoon chopped fresh ginger
- 4 garlic cloves, crushed and chopped
- 4 scallions, both white and green parts, minced
- 2 tablespoons dark soy sauce
- 1 teaspoon spicy sesame oil
- 2 cups cooking oil
- 2 cups broth (chicken, beef, or vegetable)
- 2 cups coarsely chopped chinese cabbage (bok choy or napa)

1. In a large bowl, combine the pork, ginger, garlic, scallions, soy sauce, wine, egg, cornstarch, and sesame oil and mix well.
2. Form into 4 large meatballs or 8 small meatballs, as desired.
3. In the wok, heat the cooking oil to 350°F, or until a wooden chopstick dipped into the oil causes bubbles. Fry the meatballs until evenly browned. Remove and set aside. Drain the oil.
4. Add the cabbage leaves and simmer for 5 minutes, until tender.
5. Serve the meatballs on beds of cooked cabbage.

Buffalo Chicken Pot Stickers

Prep time: 10 minutes | Cook time: 20 minutes | Serves 24

- 4 tablespoons oil
- 1 medium onion, finely chopped
- 2 stalks celery, chopped
- 1 pound ground chicken
- ½ cup Frank's hot sauce
- 2 cups cheddar cheese, shredded
- Salt and black pepper, to taste
- 48 dumpling wrappers

1. Sauté onion and celery with oil in a Mandarin wok until soft.
2. Stir in chicken and cook until it is golden-brown.
3. Add hot sauce, cheddar cheese, black pepper, and salt.
4. Mix well and cook this filling for 5 minutes.
5. Allow the filling to cool and spread the dumpling wrappers on the working surface.
6. Meanwhile, heat about 2 tablespoons oil in a skillet.
7. Sear the dumpling for 2 minutes until golden.
8. Serve warm.

Scallion Pancakes

Prep time: 40 minutes | Cook time: 10 minutes | Serves 4

- 2 cups all-purpose flour, plus additional for dusting
- ¾ cup warm water
- ½ cup cold water
- 2 to 4 tablespoons vegetable or peanut oil, plus additional as needed
- 3 or 4 scallions, thinly sliced

1. In a large bowl, mix the flour and warm water together to form a dough. Work the cold water into the dough, a little bit at a time, until a smooth and not too sticky dough forms.
2. Roll out the dough onto a floured cutting board. Divide it into four equal pieces.
3. Roll each piece of dough into a level circle, 7 to 8 inches in diameter. Brush the top of each circle lightly with some of the oil. Top each circle with one quarter of the scallions.
4. Heat your wok over medium-low heat. Using about ½ to 1 tablespoon of oil, lightly fry each dough circle until golden brown, 2 to 3 minutes per side.
5. Serve warm with Sesame Dipping Sauce or regular soy sauce.

Chapter 10

Appetizers and Dessert

Thai Iced Tea

Prep time: 15 minutes | Cook time: 25 minutes | Serves 4

4 cups (960 ml) water
½ cup (95 g) packaged thai tea mix
1 cup (200 g) sugar
3–4 tbsp (45–60 ml) half-and-half

1. Bring the water to a boil in a medium saucepan. Stir in the Thai tea mix. Simmer it over medium-low heat for about 20 minutes. Stir in the sugar, to taste. Strain the tea through a sieve lined with cheesecloth. Chill it down in the fridge for a few hours. It will keep, refrigerated, for up to 2 weeks.
2. When ready to serve, fill a tall glass with ice. Pour the tea over the ice, leaving about ½ inch (13 mm) of room at the top. Top with half-and-half and insert straw. Make sure the drinker uses that straw to mix the half-and-half thoroughly before drinking.

Candyfloss Sweet Potato

Prep time: 5 minutes | Cooking time: 25 minutes | Serves 4

- 4 medium sweet potatoes (1lb /454g)
- 3 tablespoons cornstarch
- 1 tablespoon canola oil, plus more for deep-frying
- ½ cup granulated sugar
- ¼ cup water
- 1 tablespoon distilled white vinegar

1. Peel and quarter the sweet potatoes lengthwise. Roll-cut them to form irregular bite-size pieces. Bring a medium pot of water to a boil over high heat. Drop the sweet potato into the water and cook them for 3 minutes. Drain the pieces of sweet potato in a colander.
2. In a large bowl, toss the pieces of sweet potato in the cornstarch.
3. Eat this dish right away before the sugar coating hardens.

Dairy-Free Banana Fudge Pops

Prep time: 5 minutes, plus time to set in the freezer | Cook time: 20 minutes | Serves 6

- 1 (13-ounce) can full-fat coconut milk
- ⅓ cup raw cacao powder
- ⅔ cup raw cashews
- 2 teaspoons maca root powder (optional)
- 1 tablespoon collagen powder or unflavored gelatin powder
- pinch sea salt
- 3 tablespoons coconut, granulated, or brown sugar
- 2 bananas, sliced

1. Combine all the ingredients in a blender and blend until smooth.
2. Pour into ice pop molds.
3. Freeze and enjoy!

Sesame Balls

Prep time: 10 minutes | Cook time: 15 minutes | Serves 8

- 1 ½ cups glutinous rice flour
- 1/3 cup granulated sugar
- ¼ cup boiling water
- ¼ cup water
- 7 ounces lotus paste or red bean paste
- ¼ cup sesame seeds
- 4 cups peanut oil, for frying

1. Mix sugar, ¼ cup rice flour, and ¼ cup warm water in a bowl and leave for 5 minutes.
2. Stir in remaining water, and remaining rice flour.
3. Mix well, cover the dough, and leave it for 30 minutes.
4. Deep fry the sesame balls until golden-brown.
5. Serve.

Amber Walnuts

Prep time: 5 minutes | Cooking time: 20 minutes | Serves 4

- 2 cups walnuts
- ½ cup granulated sugar
- 1½ cups canola oil
- 2 tablespoons toasted white sesame seeds

1. Bring a medium pot of water to a boil over high heat. Add the walnuts and blanch them for 3 minutes. Drain the walnuts in a colander.
2. Store the walnuts in a sealed glass jar in the pantry for up to 1 week.

Wok Fried Peanuts

Prep time: 10 minutes | Cook time: 2 minutes | Serves 4

- 6 ounces shelled raw red-skin peanuts
- 2 tablespoons neutral-flavored oil
- sea salt, to taste

1. Sauté peanuts with oil and salt in a Cantonese wok for 2 minutes.
2. Serve.

Mung Bean Cakes

Prep time: 15 minutes | Cooking time: 50 minutes | Serves 6

- 1½ cups peeled dried mung beans
- 1 cup granulated sugar
- ½ cup corn oil, or another very mild-flavored oil
- Flat-bottomed stainless steel or bamboo steamer with a large pot
- Moon cake mold

1. Soak the beans for 12 hours or overnight. Drain them completely.
2. Place the beans on a deep plate in a steamer. Heat the steamer over high heat until it comes to full steam. Reduce the heat to medium and steam for 30 minutes. Press a bean between your fingers; if it crumbles, it's cooked.
3. Serve the cakes either fresh or chilled for a better taste. If you're not eating them right away, store in an airtight container in the refrigerator for up to 3 days.

Green Tea Ice Cream

Prep time: 15 minutes | Cook time: 25 minutes | Makes 1 quart (946 ml)

- 2 cups (480 ml) heavy cream
- 2 cups (480 ml) half-and-half
- 1 tsp vanilla extract
- 9 egg yolks
- ¾ cup (150 g) sugar
- 2 tbsp (20 g) green tea powder

1. In a medium saucepan over medium heat, combine the cream, half-and-half and vanilla, stirring occasionally to make sure the mixture doesn't scorch on the bottom. When the cream mixture reaches a simmer (do not let it boil), remove from the heat.
2. Quickly remove it from the heat and whisk in the green tea powder until completely combined. Place the contents into a metal bowl and chill in the refrigerator until completely cool, about 4 hours to overnight. Now follow the directions of your ice cream maker of choice and enjoy!

Coconut Sticky Rice with Mango

Prep time: 15 minutes | Cook time: 25 minutes | Serves 4-6

- 3 cups (640 g) thai sweet rice
- 2 cups (480 ml) coconut milk
- 1–1½ cups (200–300 g) granulated sugar
- 1 tsp salt
- 4 manila mangoes, sliced into thin long pieces

1. Soak the sweet rice covered in water for at least 3 hours, preferably overnight.
2. Transfer the soaked rice into a bamboo basket. The rice should sit on the bottom of the basket. Add 4 cups (960 ml) of water into the steamer pot. Heat the water on high until it's boiling.
3. Insert the basket into the pot and cover it for 10 minutes. Flip the rice once and let it steam for another 10 minutes.
4. Heat the coconut milk, sugar and salt in a small saucepan until simmering, then remove it from the heat. Reserve ¼ cup (60 ml) and fold the remaining coconut sauce into rice. Cover the rice for 30 minutes.
5. When ready to serve, drizzle the reserved coconut sauce over the rice, and serve with very ripe mangoes or any fruit in season.

Hakka Spice Popcorn

Prep time: 10 minutes | Cook time: 10 minutes | Serves 4

For The Spice Blend

- 1 whole star anise, seeds removed and husks discarded
- 6 green cardamom pods, seeds removed and husks discarded
- 4 whole cloves
- 4 black peppercorns
- ½ teaspoon ground turmeric
- ⅛ teaspoon ground cayenne pepper

For The Popcorn

- 2 tablespoons vegetable oil
- ½ cup popcorn kernels
- Kosher salt

To Make The Spice Blend

1. Add the ground cinnamon, ginger, turmeric, and cayenne pepper and stir to combine. Set aside.

To Make The Popcorn

2. Heat a wok over medium-high heat until it just begins to smoke. Pour in the vegetable oil and ghee and swirl to coat the wok. Add 2 popcorn kernels to the wok and cover. Once they pop, add the rest of the kernels and cover. Shake constantly until the popping stops and remove from the heat.

Volume Equivalents (Dry)

US STANDARD	METRIC (APPROXIMATE)
1/8 teaspoon	0.5 mL
1/4 teaspoon	1 mL
1/2 teaspoon	2 mL
3/4 teaspoon	4 mL
1 teaspoon	5 mL
1 tablespoon	15 mL
1/4 cup	59 mL
1/2 cup	118 mL
3/4 cup	177 mL
1 cup	235 mL
2 cups	475 mL
3 cups	700 mL
4 cups	1 L

Weight Equivalents

US STANDARD	METRIC (APPROXIMATE)
1 ounce	28 g
2 ounces	57 g
5 ounces	142 g
10 ounces	284 g
15 ounces	425 g
16 ounces (1 pound)	455 g
1.5 pounds	680 g
2 pounds	907 g

Volume Equivalents (Liquid)

US STANDARD	US STANDARD (OUNCES)	METRIC (APPROXIMATE)
2 tablespoons	1 fl.oz.	30 mL
1/4 cup	2 fl.oz.	60 mL
1/2 cup	4 fl.oz.	120 mL
1 cup	8 fl.oz.	240 mL
1 1/2 cup	12 fl.oz.	355 mL
2 cups or 1 pint	16 fl.oz.	475 mL
4 cups or 1 quart	32 fl.oz.	1 L
1 gallon	128 fl.oz.	4 L

Temperatures Equivalents

FAHRENHEIT(F)	CELSIUS(C) APPROXIMATE)
225 °F	107 °C
250 °F	120 ° °C
275 °F	135 °C
300 °F	150 °C
325 °F	160 °C
350 °F	180 °C
375 °F	190 °C
400 °F	205 °C
425 °F	220 °C
450 °F	235 °C
475 °F	245 °C
500 °F	260 °C

Appendix 2 The Dirty Dozen and Clean Fifteen

The Environmental Working Group (EWG) is a nonprofit, nonpartisan organization dedicated to protecting human health and the environment Its mission is to empower people to live healthier lives in a healthier environment. This organization publishes an annual list of the twelve kinds of produce, in sequence, that have the highest amount of pesticide residue-the Dirty Dozen-as well as a list of the fifteen kinds ofproduce that have the least amount of pesticide residue-the Clean Fifteen.

THE DIRTY DOZEN	

The 2016 Dirty Dozen includes the following produce. These are considered among the year's most important produce to buy organic:

Strawberries	Spinach
Apples	Tomatoes
Nectarines	Bell peppers
Peaches	Cherry tomatoes
Celery	Cucumbers
Grapes	Kale/collard greens
Cherries	Hot peppers

The Dirty Dozen list contains two additional itemskale/collard greens and hot peppers-because they tend to contain trace levels of highly hazardous pesticides.

THE CLEAN FIFTEEN	

The least critical to buy organically are the Clean Fifteen list. The following are on the 2016 list:

Avocados	Papayas
Corn	Kiw
Pineapples	Eggplant
Cabbage	Honeydew
Sweet peas	Grapefruit
Onions	Cantaloupe
Asparagus	Cauliflower
Mangos	

Some of the sweet corn sold in the United States are made from genetically engineered (GE) seedstock. Buy organic varieties of these crops to avoid GE produce.

Appendix 3 Index

Grace Kim

Printed in Great Britain
by Amazon

34030046R00044